black roses

ariel day

Contents

jay – thank you for always being there xx

foreword

these are all the words i left unsaid...

illusions

i was love with the thought of you

and you were in love with

the thought of me

- *is there really a difference?*

opposing forces

i was in love with a fantasy
and you were in love with a fairy tale
and maybe that's what drew us together
and pulled us apart

manic pixie dream girl

i was in love with
the idea
of being the kind of girl
you could be in love with

parallel universes

it took me years to realize
i wasn't in love with you.

i was in love with
– *in another life*

long term memory

i think about people
5 years later
and i wonder
does it make me pathetic?

does it make me pathetic
to dream of you
when you've probably forgotten
about me?

adjustment disorder

i'm learning to get used to normal
to boys who respect me
who listen to me
who get back to me

i'm getting used to
boys who don't say i love you
on the second date
and talk about marriage
on the third

i'm getting used to
bringing home boys
my parents would like

my therapist would like

my cat would like

i'm trying to get used to

a new start

a new life

a new me

i'm trying to get used to

not seeing you

in my dreams

in my grandparents' house

in my veins

but it's hard to get used to

not hearing you in certain phrases

or in the way

someone compliments someone

it's hard getting used to

not wondering

what you would say
when the topic turns
to love

it's hard
not hearing
your voice in my ear
whispering
like a ghost
and feeling
your vibrations
in my soul.

- *i'm not ready to forget*

heretic

i never understood
why you believed in god
until you left

god is an answer
to the question of nothingness
of filling the void
of meaninglessness

now that i

have to make sense

of life without you

i understand

that's why you believed in god,

and why i believed in you.

- i still don't believe in god

small moments

i've always found it interesting
how the smallest moments
can be the happiest
- *i still remember that phone call*

pointless questions

everyone i've ever loved
i knew it the first time i met them

i ask myself
am i a good judge of character
or just incredibly stubborn?

i ask myself these questions
but i already know the answers.

games

i love people
who bring out the parts of me
i keep hidden

i hide myself
like a child playing hide and seek

i don't know what i want more—
to hide
or for someone to find me

- *i want both*

unconditional

sometimes i think of my future daughter
and all the things i'll tell her.

i'll tell her she's beautiful
i'll tell her i understand

i'll ask her about the boys she likes
and the girls who are mean.

i'll tell her i'll listen
to the thoughts she keeps to herself

i'll tell her she's a good person
i'll tell her she belongs

just not with them

i'll tell her she'll always belong
with me

i'll tell her that i'll always listen
and that my love is unconditional

i'll talk to her
about shame
and self hatred

i'll tell her that
shame is a poison
that rots you from the inside
that secrets
don't protect you
they trap you like quicksand

i'll reach out my hand

and tell her

there's nothing you

could ever say

that would make me

not love you.

- things i wish my mother had told me

daddy issues

i still remember
when you told me
that i was getting fat
and asked me
if i 'really needed that candy?'
i told you i didn't.

i swore to myself
that i would show you
and i did

but all i showed you
was the lengths i would go to
for your approval

and the lengths you would go

to it from me.

i eat all the candy i want now.

\- *it wasn't worth it*

"joke"

"men are trash"
i say it as a joke
at least
i think i do

my best friend
says maybe i'm not straight
i tell her i am

but
if hating some men
means you're not straight
i guess i'm a circle

i try to not hate anyone

i don my armor and tell myself

no one can hurt me

but i am wrong

because my armor is too tight

and i am suffocating

from the inside out

and now the only person

i can hate

is myself.

sweet antifreeze

when i was six years old
my dad was stung by a blue bottle jellyfish
it was beautiful
i've seen my dad cry twice
when my grandma died
and when he was stung that day

when i was 13 years old
i got a book about snakes for christmas
it said snake venom
can taste sweet

two years ago

i heard about a man who poisoned his wife with
antifreeze

for weeks he laced her drinks with the sweet
liquid

and she had no idea

one month ago i asked myself

why do i keep going back to you?

that's when i remembered the jellyfish

the snakes

and the antifreeze

and it all made sense.

cross to bear

the worst kind of pain
is the kind you can't share
because you know
that sharing it
would make it so much worse.

virtue ethics

i want to be the bigger person
and be happy
for you
for her
for your new life

but i'm not.

i hope you think of me
when the sun rises
and sets.
when you take your first sip of whiskey
and when you take your last.

i hope you think of me
when the lilies bloom
and the first snowflake falls.

i hope you think of me
every time you fuck her

and if that makes me a bad person?
i don't care

savior complex

you once told me
that every time i opened up to you
you felt a high
you told me you liked the brokenness
the rawness
the realness
you told me
you liked being my savior
but you never told me
you liked being my tormentor,
too.

the most popular guy at the funeral

when your grandma died
13 of your friends
came to her funeral.

i remember thinking
how special you must be
to have so many close friends.
and then
on a bus one day
i asked you
to name 20 things i liked
and you couldn't name one

that's when i understood.

naive cynic

you called me your future wife
after 3 dates
and introduced me to all your friends
you called me cynical
too afraid to commit

we broke up
and
9 months later
you were engaged.

i still can't figure out
whether i broke it
or if it was broken from the start.

paradox

why are the easiest
people to hate
also
the easiest to love?

to my grave

high on cocaine
you told me a secret
i swore to keep.

i don't owe you anything
anymore
but i've kept it.

i don't know
if that's loyalty
or a futile attempt
to preserve what's left.

she may have your physical presence

but i still have this

a snapshot in time

of vulnerability

of connection

of what could have been

soulmates

i believe in soulmates
a completely unscientific
concept, i know.

i met my soulmate when i was 17
i'm 29 now
and sometimes i wonder
am i romanticizing the past?

but then i think back
and i remember
how he made me feel

he saw me

the way i wanted
to see myself

i haven't felt like that since
or seen that girl.

i miss her.

homesick

we were drunk one night
and he told me
he wasn't the smartest guy
or the best looking
but he could promise me one thing—
he'd love me more
than any man could.

his words have haunted me since that day.

i've loved other men
and other men have loved me
but none of them
felt like home
the way he did.

blissful ignorance

you need openness
for acceptance
but cynicism
closes you up.

i'm open to being open
but being open
is not the same as believing.

and once belief is shattered
you can't get it back.

- *things i wish i could unsee*

ghost ships

sometimes i wonder
if i miss him
or if i miss
what i can't have

i think of him when i'm lonely
and remind myself
good things exist.

he's the anchor i cling to
but he's gone.

do i want to make it back to shore?

sometimes i wonder

if i'd rather stay in the ocean

free

staring down infinite waters

and wondering

what's past the horizon

afterword

thank you for joining me on this journey.

you're not alone.

– ariel

about ariel

ariel is a writer from vancouver, canada.

she likes green tea, exploring old churches, and going on hikes with her jack russell terrier beau.

she writes about themes of love, loss, and mental health.